W9-APK-707

Lions & Tigers

and other Big Cats

Dalmatian
KIDS

The DALMATIAN KIDS name and logo are trademarks of
Dalmatian Publishing Group, Atlanta, Georgia 30329.

Published by Dalmatian Kids, an imprint of Dalmatian Publishing Group.
Text Copyright © 2007 by Dalmatian Publishing Group, LLC
Art Copyright © 2007 Edizioni Larus S.p.A.

Printed in the U.S.A. • 1-40373-433-X
07 08 09 B&M 9 8 7 6 5 4 3 2 1

Lion

The lion is the largest, strongest cat in the African *savanna* (grassland region). The male has a thick, yellow or brown mane.

Lions live in groups called *prides* that have females, cubs younger than two years old, and a few males. These males control the pride and mark its territory every day with scent marks and loud roars.

When it's very hot, lions rest near water, in the shade, or in rocky areas. Sometimes they nap on tree branches.

Did You Know
When a male loses to a stronger lion, the winner takes over the pride.

Baby Lions

When she's ready to have a baby, the female goes alone into the *bush* (land thickly-grown with underbrush and trees). There she has up to three spotted cubs. A few days later, when the babies can walk, the mother brings them back to the pride. For two years the cubs learn the rules of the group and how to hunt. Then the males leave.

Mother lions love their cubs. A baby lion can play with its mother's tail, and every part of her body, but she never seems to mind.

CREATURE FEATURE:
A male lion sleeps about twenty hours a day and hunts at night.

What does it eat?
Antelope, warthogs, and gazelles. And because they hunt in groups, lions can catch big animals, like buffalo.

Leopard

The leopard is a big cat that lives in the forest and the African savanna. Its fur, with dark spots shaped like rings on a tan background, makes it almost invisible against the forest background.

Leopards are good climbers that live alone in trees where it's safe.

Baby Leopards

The female has one cub in a cave or thick forest. For two years she teaches it to hunt and escape from lions. Then the young leopard is on its own.

Did You Know?

Because of the leopard's beautiful spotted coat, humans have hunted it almost to *extinction* (dying out). Leopards are now protected by law.

CREATURE FEATURE: The leopard is so strong that it can lift animals heavier than itself just by using its teeth!

What does it eat?
Mostly medium-sized animals such as gazelles and impalas—and even baboons in the treetops! Also small mammals like foxes, jackals, monkeys, porcupines, and even birds.

5

Cheetah

The cheetah is a slender cat with long limbs. It has a golden coat with black spots that help it blend into the background.

A cheetah's head is small for its body. Its teeth are weak, and it has smaller *canines* (pointed teeth) than other cats. But the cheetah runs very fast, and can climb onto boulders and dead trees to get a better view of its prey.

What does it eat?

Gazelles and other animals that run quickly. This cat sprints like lightning! If its prey tries to zigzag away, the cheetah changes direction. His extra long tail keeps him balanced during sharp turns, and his claws help him hold onto the ground when running.

Did You Know?

When it sprints, the cheetah burns up all of its energy. If it doesn't catch its prey right away, it gives up.

Baby Cheetahs

A female cheetah usually has three cubs in the dense forest. When she hunts, the mother hides her cubs in the thick grass until she comes back to nurse. When she's near the cubs, she stays on guard against lions and hyenas who might try to steal them.

The mother tenderly cares for her cubs and teaches them how to hunt.

When they are one year old, young cheetahs can take care of themselves. They set out alone in the savanna.

Baby cheetahs have a long, pale *mantle* (covering) from head to tail. When they grow up, they shed this fur.

CREATURE FEATURE:
The cheetah is the world's fastest mammal. It can sprint 70 mph!

The Siberian tiger is the largest cat in the world. It can weigh 700 pounds and be 7 feet long from the tip of its nose to the end of its tail. Just the tail can be longer than 3 feet!

The Siberian tiger has dark brown stripes on a reddish-orange coat. In winter, its fur gets lighter, and a white strip spreads under its muzzle and cheeks and all along its belly.

This tiger likes low, mountainous areas. He hides in forests near large rivers and loves to take cover among the river reeds, since they disguise him.

Siberian tigers like to live alone. Only during mating time, when tigers form pairs, do they live in the same territory with other tigers.

> **CREATURE FEATURE:**
> A Siberian tiger is very strong. He can carry a 300-pound wild boar, and even swim with it across a river!

Baby Siberian Tigers

Three cubs are usually born in a safe den. The mother protects and nurses them for a long time.

Siberian tiger cubs stay with their mother until they are two or three years old. They spend a lot of time playing with each other and learning from their mother how to find food.

Did You Know?

Tigers don't usually attack people. However, if a tiger is wounded and cannot hunt wild animals, he might turn on a human.

What does it eat?

Wild boars, deer, and elk. This tiger will even attack bears! He is a skilled hunter, slinking along the ground between the tall grasses as he hunts. The tiger uses the heavy weight of his body to knock another animal down to the ground when running.

9

Snow Leopard

The snow leopard of central and northern Asia is a very large cat. It can weigh up to 120 pounds.

To protect itself in its cold mountain home, the snow leopard has thick, smoky gray fur. In the winter, this fur grows up to 5 inches long under its belly! Its ears are tiny to reduce the area exposed to cold air.

Snow leopards live alone in high mountains. In fact, in summer, snow leopards live in altitudes up to 19,600 feet. In the winter they go down into valleys.

What does it eat?

Large animals from the mountains: *ibexes* (goats with long horns), Asiatic *mouflons* (wild sheep), and young yaks. Also, smaller animals, like *marmots* (bushy-tailed rodents) and *pikas* (mammals similar to rabbits).

CREATURE FEATURE:
Snow leopards are great hunters. To catch partridges and grouses, they can make 50-foot leaps!

Baby Snow Leopards

The mother snow leopard gives birth in a crevice in the rocks. She has mostly litters of two. The mother usually covers the den with soft *pelts* (animal skins) and her own long fur.

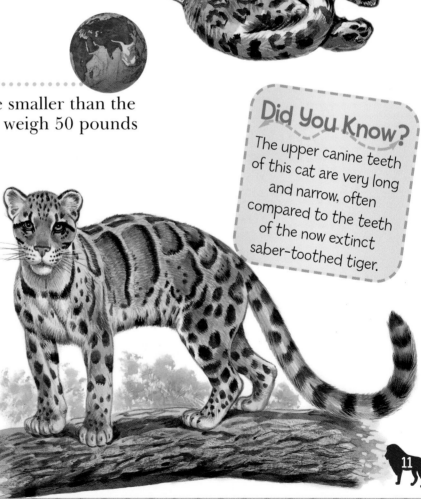

Clouded Leopard

Clouded leopards of Asia are smaller than the snow leopard. In fact, they weigh 50 pounds at the very most.

Their coats are pale yellow or tan colored, with large dark spots. The cloudy effect of their fur makes them invisible in the trees of the tropical forests where they live. This leopard is a very skilled tree climber and is one of the only felines capable of descending trunks head first. By 11 weeks, clouded leopard cubs are already excellent tree climbers and spend most of their time high up in the branches.

Did You Know?

The upper canine teeth of this cat are very long and narrow, often compared to the teeth of the now extinct saber-toothed tiger.

Bengal Tiger

With its fancy striped coat, the Bengal of India and south-central Asia has earned the nickname "royal tiger." Males are about 10 feet long and can weigh up to 600 pounds; females are slightly smaller.

The Bengal is in danger of dying out today. Centuries of hunting by man, and the destruction of the tiger's home, have almost destroyed this beautiful animal.

aby Bengal Tigers

female tiger can have three cubs
t a time. Cubs stay with their
nother for two years. Then the
nales leave their mother's home
o find their own. Females usually
ay behind.

What does it eat?

Deer, pigs, and buffalo. They usually avoid humans, but when forced to live near humans, they can still be "man-eaters." This huge cat is a perfect hunter because its stripes hide it in the underbrush.

13

Asian Lion

Today only about 300 Asian lions exist in the Gir Forest Natural Park. Compared with their African "cousins," Asian lions have lighter, thinner fur. Their behavior is different, too. In Asia, the prides are composed only of females and cubs. Males live alone or in small groups. Unlike African lions, the Asian males also hunt alone, without females, hiding in the cover of the forest before they ambush prey.

CREATURE FEATURE:
Young Asian lions are blind at birth. For the first eight weeks, they feed only on mother's milk and are not able to hunt until they are about one and a half years old.

Did You Know?
A baby lion's spotted fur helps it hide and survive in the bush.

Black Panther

The famous black panther is really… a leopard! Its spots are hard to see because the background color of its coat is black, too. Black leopards can be found in forests, while yellow leopards live in open areas. However, black and yellow leopards can be born in the same litter! The panther's biggest enemy is the tiger, which is bigger and stronger.

What does it eat?
Deer and antelope are favorites.
But a panther will prey on just about
any animal, like monkeys,
goats, and calves.

Lynx

The lynx is the largest wild cat in Europe. It lives hidden in the dense forest, is a skilled tree climber, and can swim across rivers.

It has good senses, but its large yellow eyes have created a myth that the cat has extremely sharp eyesight: "eyes like a lynx."

Baby Lynxes

A female lynx gives birth to blind, helpless kittens in its den. The mother takes care of them for five months, teaching them how to hunt until they are one year old.

What does it eat?

Hares, foxes, squirrels, deer, antelope, and livestock. In the winter, its large paws keep it from sinking into the snow so it can catch prey.

16

Canadian Lynx

The silvery-gray or reddish coat of the Canadian lynx is so thick and long that this animal is the most beautiful of all the lynxes. It has fluffy tufts on its ears, and a fringe of fur on its cheeks, with spots along its back and sides.

Because these lynxes have thick, light fur in winter, they're hard to see against the snow.

Baby Canadian Lynxes

In spring, the female goes to a den hollowed out of a dense thicket, and gives birth to two or three blind, helpless cubs. They open their eyes after sixteen days and nurse for five months. Their mother defends them and teaches them hunting for a year.

CREATURE FEATURE:
Canadian lynxes can snatch small birds in flight!

Bobcat

The bobcat is sometimes called a "red lynx," but bobcats differ from the common lynx. A bobcat is smaller, its feet are unprotected by fur, and the tufts on its ears are shorter. Its tail is longer, too, with black bands, a white underside, and a black tip.

Baby Bobcats

A female bobcat makes a den—usually under a boulder, in a hollow trunk, in the thick underbrush, or among the rocks. Then she lines it with moss and leaves. Within two months, up to six cubs are born.

  The mother and cubs stay in the den for several months until the cubs stop nursing. Then, in winter, the mother sends them off to fend for themselves. A nine-month-old bobcat kit can already hunt by itself!

What does it eat?
The bobcat is nocturnal, sleeping during the day and moving around at night. Its favorite prey is the jackrabbit, but it also catches rodents, small birds, and deer.

18

Ocelot

Ocelots are called "painted leopards." No two look alike! Their coats can be tawny-yellow, gray, or reddish-gray, and are covered with coffee-colored blotches ringed with black.

The ocelot is one of the largest cats in the Americas.

Baby Ocelots

The female ocelot usually has one or two young. For her babies, the mother makes a bed of leaves in the hollow of a tree, in an abandoned den, or in a cave hidden in the forest.

Ocelot cubs look and act just like kittens. Cubs raised by humans will purr like domestic cats!

What does it eat?
Rabbits and mice, as well as iguanas and lizards. Along riverbeds, ocelots catch frogs, crabs, small turtles, and fish.

Jaguar

The jaguar is the largest cat in the Western Hemisphere. It can weigh up to 265 pounds! A jaguar's coat is yellow, covered with dark spots and rosettes that are different on every animal.

With its stocky body and short limbs, the jaguar can move easily in the forest. It's a skilled tree climber and excellent swimmer. Jaguars avoid mountainous regions; they like vast, marshy forests. They mark their hunting territories by scratching tree trunks and spraying their scent.

Some say the name jaguar comes from a South-American Indian word meaning "beast that kills in one bound." An expert tree climber, jaguars often leap down onto prey below.

Baby Jaguars

Females usually have two or three cubs in a thicket. The blind, helpless young ones stay hidden for two months; then they go out to search for food.

Cubs stay with their mother until they are two years old. They learn the secrets of hunting, such as how to find turtle eggs hidden in sandy river-banks, how to catch crabs and fish in the swamps, and how to chase monkeys and sloths without falling from the treetops!

What does it eat?
Deer, large rodents, fish, and reptiles. With a great leap, the jaguar pounces on the victim and kills it by biting its neck. After seeing a herd, the jaguar attacks the animal farthest from the group and tries to drag the victim as fast as possible up a tree.

Did You Know?
A jaguar can catch fish by tapping the surface of the water with its tail. The sound is like the plop of fruit or a large insect falling into the water. When fish swim up for a meal, the jaguar harpoons them with its claws.

21

Puma

CREATURE FEATURE:
A puma can act just like a domestic cat! It washes its face with a paw after licking it with its tongue, rolls on its back, and eats like a house cat.

What does it eat?
Big prey, such as swamp deer and the guanaco, a relative of the llama, as well as smaller animals, like hares and large rodents.

The puma is a large cat, more similar to domestic cats than are big African felines. It can weigh from 75 to 240 pounds because it adapts to different habitats.

The color of a puma's coat varies, too. North American pumas have silvery gray fur, the ones at the Equator are rusty red, and those in the far south are shades of gray.

Baby Pumas

The female puma has her babies in a sheltered place, like a cave. They are born mostly in summer.

The mother can have five cubs at a time. The babies are helpless, opening their eyes after ten days. They nurse for three months and stay with their mother for about two years.

North American Puma (Cougar)

The cougar is a large feline that looks like a lioness; in fact, sometimes it's called a mountain lion. However, its body is skinnier and it has a smaller head. Both males and females have short, tawny fur.

Cougars adapt well to the places where they live. They can handle the cold in Canada or the extreme heat of California's deserts. During the day, they hide in thick vegetation or in trees. They hunt at night.

23

Baby Cougars

The female bears two or three cubs in her den. The young are blind, weigh only about a pound, and are completely helpless. The mother protects them, nurses them, and keeps them clean by licking them with her rough tongue. After a month and a half, she brings them their first prey. Babies stay with their mother until they're two years old.

CREATURE FEATURE:
Cougar cubs are covered with dark spots and have banded tails to hide them from enemies, like wolves. At about five months, they begin to lose their spots, and at 10 months, their coats are identical to that of an adult cougar.